# PABLO
# NERUDA

# LUIS POIROT

# PABLO NERUDA

## Absence and Presence

Translations by Alastair Reid

W·W·Norton & Company

New York     London

Excerpts from *Extravagaria* by Pablo Neruda, translated by Alastair Reid. Translation copyright © 1976, 1977 by Farrar, Straus and Giroux, Inc. Reprinted by permission of the Estate of Pablo Neruda, the translator, and the publishers, Jonathan Cape Ltd. and Farrar, Straus and Giroux, Inc.

Excerpts from *Fully Empowered* by Pablo Neruda, translated by Alastair Reid. Translation copyright © 1967, 1969, 1970, 1975 by Alastair Reid. Reprinted by permission of the publishers, Souvenir Press Ltd. and Farrar, Straus and Giroux, Inc.

Excerpts from *Isla Negra* by Pablo Neruda, translated by Alastair Reid. Translation copyright © 1970, 1979, 1981 by Alastair Reid. Reprinted by permission of the publishers, Souvenir Press Ltd. and Farrar, Straus and Giroux, Inc.

Excerpts from *Memoirs* by Pablo Neruda, translated by Hardie St. Martin. Translation copyright © 1976, 1977 by Farrar, Straus and Giroux, Inc. Reprinted by permission of the publishers, Souvenir Press Ltd. and Farrar, Straus and Giroux, Inc.

Excerpts from *Selected Poems of Pablo Neruda* reprinted by permission of the Estate of Pablo Neruda and the publishers, Jonathan Cape Ltd.

Excerpts from *Canto Ceremoniales, Canto General, Cien Sonnetos de Amor, El Mar y las Campanas, Estravagario, Geographie, Isla Negra, La Baracola, Navagaciones y Regressos, Odas Elementales, Plenos Poceres, Tercer Libro de Odas, Tercera Residencia,* and *Viajes,* all by Pablo Neruda, and *My Life with Pablo Neruda* by Matilde Urratia reprinted by permission of Fundación Pablo Neruda.

The text of this book is composed in New Century Schoolbook, with display type set in Bodoni Book. Composition by The Maple-Vail Book Manufacturing Group. Manufacturing by Amilcare Pizzi S.P.A., Italy. Originally designed by Hernan Parada (IDEAS/Fontenay s-Bois—France)

First Edition

Library of Congress Cataloging-in-Publication Data

Poirot, Luis.
    [Neruda. English]
    Pablo Neruda : absence and presence / by Luis Poirot ; translations
by Alastair Reid.—1st ed.
        p.   cm.
    Translation of: Neruda.
    1. Neruda, Pablo, 1904–1973—Homes and haunts—Chile—Isla Negra—
Pictorial works.   2. Neruda, Pablo, 1904–1973—Friends and
associates.   3. Neruda, Pablo 1904–1973—Portraits.   4. Isla Negra
(Chile)—Description and travel—Views.   I. Title.
    PQ8097.N4Z72513   1990
    861—dc20
    [B]                                                89–33112

ISBN 0-393-02770-8

ISBN 0-393-30643-7 {PBK}

W. W. Norton & Company, Inc., 500 Fifth Avenue, New York, N. Y. 10110
W. W. Norton & Company Ltd., 37 Great Russell Street, London WC1B 3NU

1 2 3 4 5 6 7 8 9 0

To Rogelia Vilamitjana and Carla Cristi

# Absence and Presence

I met Neruda in 1969, and a year later I went back to see him in Isla Negra. From those moments I have his portraits and very intense memories. When I returned to Chile in 1982, after nine years of absence, his widow, Matilde Urrutia, agreed to my book project and generously allowed me to roam freely through his house in Isla Negra for several days so that I could photograph it. There all the ghosts of absence and remembrance arose; the writing on the fence, that huge collective book, made me certain that the country remembered. Almost fortuitously, magical and moving stories about Neruda began to seek me out.

I returned to Barcelona and there, in the stillness of the darkroom, the images and emotions which touch this book began to appear. In the following two years, I went back to Chile, visited Matilde, the fence and the witnesses.

During the summer months of 1986, I immersed myself in reading the complete works of Neruda, and in his voice I found two paragraphs that showed me how to structure my book:

> Tyranny cuts off the singer's head,
> but the voice from the bottom of the well
> returns to the secret streams of the earth
> and rises out of nowhere through the mouths of the people.

That was precisely the impression that I had received in my visits to Chile: Neruda, a forbidden name, was an emblem of hope and of what was best in us as a people as we confronted the daily horror of the dictatorship.

The other lines were:

> There's no forgetting, there's no winter
> that will wipe your name, shining brother, from
> the lips of the people.

In a photograph which I had taken of the fence months before, there was a line that the wind and rain had already begun to erase: "There's no forgetting."

It was clear to me that the dialogue between the poet and his people continued.

I searched for a way to make a book that could be followed by either reading the text or looking at the photographs, or, ideally, by doing both things at the same time.

The sequence of the photographs was determined by looking for a visual language that on the one hand would give them a dramatic narrative structure, and in the case of Neruda's houses, would make the camera seem to be the eyes of the owner wandering about looking at the abandoned objects.

Matilde Urrutia was the first one to help me find some of Neruda's old friends, some of them completely forgotten, like Jorge Saure—perhaps the most important photographer in Chile.

---

Little by little, from friend to friend, from poem to poem, the book took shape.

Shortly before she died, Matilde urged me to photograph the house in Valparaiso, which had been looted after the 1973 military coup and which she hadn't wanted to repair so that it could become, according to her words, a "testimony to barbarism." Two days after her death, the mythical house of Isla Negra was closed and taken over by the military. The photographs which I had taken are the only documentation of that house since September 1973—until it becomes the Neruda Museum, which will belong to all the people of Chile.

This recovery of collective memories seems imperative to me in a country which seems to remember only battles. In the time from the beginning of my search to the publication of this U.S. edition, Matilde Urrutia, Jorge Saure, Manuel Solimano, Julio Cortazar, Jose Venturelli, and others with whom I would have liked to have spoken have died.

In March 1986, when the Neruda Foundation, the legal owner of all his legacy, was still not officially recognized in Chile, its members agreed to publish an edition of 500 books. Months later, Alastair Reid, Neruda's translator and generous friend, was the person instrumental in the publication of this English version.

And that's the way that I returned to Chile permanently, choosing, perhaps, to do it holding Pablo Neruda's hand.

Luis Poirot
Santiago, Chile, January 1989

# Preface

Translated ubiquitously, with huge editions in Russian and Chinese, Neruda is probably the most read poet in history. Besides that, he had legions of friends. Only some of them were human beings; the others were plants, animals, trees, landscapes, objects of all description, and houses. Neruda appeared to live on terms of intimacy with the world of things, and to carry on secret conversations with all kinds of beings, animate and inanimate, conversations that often became poems. He lived outwardly, not inwardly. All his life he collected a great variety of things: ships-in-bottles, shells, French postcards, ships' figureheads, sextants, astrolabes, clocks, stones, books, hats, bottles. He was a passionate acquirer. But he was also a great traveler, who always returned to Chile, his roots, with a new bounty of objects picked up along the way. These growing collections needed, of course, somewhere to come to rest, but also somewhere to show themselves off. So Neruda anchored himself firmly to Chile by transforming a series of houses there into his center, his point of rest, where he kept his desk. He required of his houses only that they be in remarkable places, that they have space for his collections and his books, as well as his architectural whimsies, that they set aside a workroom for him, and that they be comfortable, humorous, and accessible to his friends. The houses were Neruda's private theaters, in which he had designed the sets, and always played the leading role. They also fulfilled early dreams Neruda had of being an architect, but a comic, surreal architect, who built to please himself.

Three houses figured largely in his life, in his poems, and in the photographs that follow: La Chascona, the house in a wild garden on the upper edge of Santiago, adjoining the zoo; La Sebastiana, the eccentric sky house he tacked onto the back of a movie theater in Valparaiso, overlooking the whole harbor; and the ocean house in Isla Negra, facing the Pacific, which Neruda kept adding to with the proceeds of each new book, and where he most fruitfully came to rest between journeys. That part of his life, from the 1950s on, in Isla Negra, Neruda called his "autumn." It was for him a time of great happiness, great fullness, of the warmly human poems of *Estravagario,* some of which grace this volume. He lent these houses his own aura, he imbued them with his own whimsical presence, so that the empty rooms invoke him, imply him, as Luis Poirot's photographs make tangibly clear to me.

In the house at Isla Negra, with the Pacific thundering below, Neruda played "armchair sailor" as he called it, hoisting his own flag of presence on a home-made yardarm; as he talked, he would often lift the sextant, or touch the stones of the fireplace or the bleached wood of the figureheads. His houses served as annexes to his head, his chosen objects extensions of his own imagination, the vocabulary of his poems, just as the sea, forever sounding outside, served as his pervasive metaphor.

Alastair Reid

# Absence

White foam, March in Isla Negra, I see
wave working on wave, the whiteness weakening
the ocean overflowing from its bottomless cup,
the still sky crisscrossed
by long slow flights of sacerdotal birds,
and the yellow comes,
the month changes color, the beard
of a seacoast autumn grows,
and I am called Pablo,
I am the same so far,
I have love, I have doubts,
I have debts,
I have the vast sea with its workers
moving wave after wave,
I am so restless that I visit
nations not yet born—
I come and go on the sea and its countries.
I know
the language of the fishbone,
the tooth of the hard fish,
chill of the latitudes,
blood of the coral, the silent
night of the whale,
for from land to land I went, exploring
estuaries, insufferable regions,
and always I returned, I found no peace—
what could I say at all without my roots?

Espuma blanca, Marzo en la Isla, veo
trabajar ola y ola, quebrarse la blancura,
desbordar el océano de su insaciable copa,
el cielo estacionario dividido
por largos lentos vuelos de aves sacerdotales
y llega el amarillo,
cambia el color del mes, crece la barba
del otoño marino,
y yo me llamo Pablo,
soy el mismo hasta ahora,
tengo amor, tengo dudas,
tengo deudas,
tengo el inmenso mar con empleados
que mueven ola y ola,
tengo tanta intemperie que visito
naciones no nacidas:
voy y vengo del mar y sus países,
conozco
los idiomas de la espina,
el diente del pez duro,
escalofrío de las latitudes,
la sangre del coral, la taciturna
noche de la ballena,
porque de tierra en tierra fui avanzando
estuario, insufribles territorios,
y siempre regresé, no tuve paz:
qué podía decir sin mis raíces?

If I die, survive me with such sheer force
that you waken the furies of the pallid and the cold,
from south to south lift your indelible eyes,
from sun to sun dream through your singing mouth.
I don't want your laughter or your steps to waver,
I don't want my heritage of joy to die.
Don't call up my person. I am absent.
Live in my absence as if in a house.
Absence is a house so vast
that inside you will pass through its walls
and hang pictures on the air.
Absence is a house so transparent
that I, lifeless, will see you, living,
and if you suffer, my love, I will die again.

Si muero sobrevíveme con tanta fuerza pura
que despiertes la furia del pálido y del frío,
de sur a sur levanta tus ojos indelebles,
de sol a sol que suene tu boca de guitarra.
No quiero que vacilen tu risa ni tus pasos,
no quiero que se muera mi herencia de alegría,
no llames a mi pecho, estoy ausente.
Vive en mi ausencia como en una casa.
Es una casa tan grande la ausencia
que pasarás en ella a través de los muros
y colgarás los cuadros en el aire.
Es una casa tan transparente la ausencia
que yo sin vida te veré vivir
y si sufres, mi amor, me moriré otra vez.

Only the shadows
know
the secrets
of closed houses,
only
the forbidden wind
and the moon that shines
on the roof

Sólo la sombra
sabe
los secretos
de las casas cerradas
sólo
el viento rechazado
y en el techo la luna que florece

The wooden girl did not arrive on foot.
She was suddenly there, resting on the tiles.
Ancient sea blooms covered up her head.
Her gaze had all the sadness of roots.

There she stayed, looking out on our lives,
our comings and goings, our crossings on the earth,
and the day slowly shedding all its petals.
She watched over us, unseeing, the wooden girl.

Maiden garlanded by ancient waves,
there she would watch us with her ruined eyes,
aware we were living in a far-off web

of time and waves and water, sounds and rain,
not knowing if we were real or if she dreamed us.
That is the story of the wooden girl.

La niña de madera no llegó caminando:
allí de pronto sentada en los ladrillos,
viejas flores del mar cubrían su cabeza,
su mirada tenía tristeza de raíces.

Allí quedó mirando nuestras vidas abiertas,
el ir y ser y andar y volver por la tierra,
el día destiñiendo sus pétalos graduales.
Vigilaba sin vernos la niña de madera.

La niña coronada por las antiguas olas,
allí miraba con sus ojos derrotados:
sabía que vivíamos en una red remota

de tiempo y agua y olas y sonidos y lluvia,
sin saber si existimos o si somos su sueño.
Esta es la historia de la muchacha de madera.

When queens and angels who came to life with you
had turned to musty dust, to sleep,
with the still honor accorded to the dead,
you took your place on the slender prow of the ship,
and, angel, queen, and wave, you stirred with life.
Men still trembled
at your noble outline with its apple breasts,
your lips still sweet, still wet
with kisses worthy of your wild mouth.

Cuando ángeles y reinas que nacieron contigo
se llenaron de musgo, durmieron destinadas
a la inmovilidad con un honor de muertos,
tú saliste a la proa delgada del navío
y ángel y reina y ola, temblor del mundo fuiste.
El estremecimiento de los hombres subía
hasta tu noble túnica con pechos de manzana
mientras tus labios eran ola dulce, humedecidos
por otros besos dignos de tu boca salvaje.

Throughout the long winter
mysterious tears roll from her glass eyes
and lie on her cheeks, not falling.
It's just the damp, say sceptics.
A miracle, say I, respectfully . . .
But why does she weep?

Durante el largo invierno algunas misteriosas lágrimas
caen de sus ojos de cristal y se quedan por sus mejillas,
sin caer. La humedad concentrada dicen los escepticidistas.
Un milagro, digo yo, con respeto...
¿ Pero por qué llora ?

. . . the sweet one,
most loved because
most wreathed in sorrow . . .

La novia
es la más amada por más dolorosa.

O lady of chipped beauty,
mistress of the ship,
setter of courses,
sea woman
of salt-stained wood,
I love your hands
hurt by the sea, your hair
motionless over eyes
that scan the round horizon,
the far reaches, the marine spring.
Your kingdom now is here, your last ship
that of my own brief life.

¡ Oh Mascarona, belleza
rota, directora del navío,
rectora del derrotero !
Dama marítima
de madera salpicada,
amo tus manos heridas
por el mar, tu cabellera
inmóvil sobre tus ojos
que escrutan el horizonte redondo,
los límites, la primavera marina.
Aquí se detuvo tu reino: tu última
nave es mi pequeña vida.

This most elegant creature journeyed on an American boat in the middle of the last century. The *Jenny Lind,* the boat was called, as were many ships after the day when the great Barnum, the first circus impresario, was bold enough to bring over the Swedish singer and present her all over the United States.

She was the first pinup, the first glamour girl, the first public sweetheart. Books, houses, boats, hotels, trains, and shops were all called after her: Jenny Lind.

Here you see her, fresh as a flower, as if about to sing.

Where the sea is concerned I am an amateur. For years I have gathered a sea-wisdom which does me little good since I set sail only on land.

Yo soy un amateur del mar. Desde hace años colecciono conocimientos que no me sirven de mucho porque navego sobre la tierra.

One chair followed me
like a poor lame horse,
stripped of both tail and mane,
with only three sad hoofs,
and I leaned against the table,
for that was the place of joy,
bread, wine, stew,
conversations with clothes,
miscellaneous functions,
and subtle occasions;
but the table was dumb
as if it had no tongue.

Alguna silla me siguió
como un pobre caballo cojo
desprovisto de cola y crines,
con tres únicas, tristes patas,
y en la mesa me recliné
porque allí estuvo la alegría,
el pan, el vino, el estofado,
las conversaciones con ropa,
con indiferentes oficios,
con casamientos delicados:
pero estaba muda la mesa
como si no tuviera lengua.

This rough head, bold and extraordinary, caught my attention in a Paris shop window. He returned my gaze, the mustachioed pirate. I thought, Could it be Morgan? He wanted out of there, back to sea, to the oceans which were his theater. He is not, however, a figurehead, but a poop statue, mounted on the quarterdeck. Years later, somewhere in the world, I found the statue's exact twin. They were both like enormous drops of water, two huge, solid drops of wood. Here he is, scanning and dominating the ocean from the wall of my house.

I know
that tiny carpenters
went in
through your delicate
throat,
flew in
on bees.
I know
that flies
brought on their backs
tools,
nails, planks,
tiny
ropes,
and so
inside the bottle
a perfect ship
took shape:
its hull the nub of its beauty,
raising its pin-sized masts . . .

Yo sé que
en tu garganta
delicada
entraron
pequeñitos
carpinteros
que volaban
en una abeja, moscas que traían
en su lomo
herramientas,
clavos, tablas,
cordeles
diminutos,
y así en una botella
el perfecto navío
fué creciendo:
el casco fué la nuez de su hermosura,
como alfileres elevó sus palos.

36

It is very appropriate, at certain times of the day or night, to look deeply into objects at rest: wheels which have traversed vast dusty spaces, bearing great cargoes of vegetables or minerals, sacks from the coalyards, barrels, baskets, the handles and grips of the carpenter's tools. They exude the touch of man and the earth as a lesson to the tormented poet. Worn surfaces, the mark hands have left on things, the aura, sometimes tragic and always wistful, of these objects, lend to reality a fascination not to be taken lightly.

The flawed confusion of human beings shows in them, the proliferation, materials used and discarded, the prints of feet and fingers, the permanent mark of humanity on the inside and outside of all objects.

That is the kind of poetry we should be after, poetry worn away as if by acid by the labor of hands, impregnated with sweat and smoke, smelling of lilies and of urine, splashed by the variety of what we do, legally or illegally.

A poetry as impure as old clothes, as a body, with its food stains and its shame; with wrinkles, observations, dreams, wakefulness, prophecies, declarations of love and hate, stupidities, shocks, idylls, political beliefs, negations, doubts affirmations, taxes.

This Guillermina turned up in Peru, from where I don't know. I heard from my friends about a figure in a Lima suburb, in a remote place. They were vague—it could be a ship's figurehead, it could be a saint. I left my friends on the corner of that twisting street and went to look. I was drawn by her beauty, by her boldness; and then, when I saw her shining nakedness, I called to my friends on the corner: "Well, at least she is no saint!"

. . . and I did not weep
because my dead brother
was as beautiful in death as in his life.

y no lloré
porque mi hermano muerto
era tan bello en muerte como en vida.

I goggle at doors,
I poke through
curtains,
I buy small
useless
objects.

Paso mirando puertas,
atravieso
cortinas,
compro pequeñas
cosas
inservibles.

Este recinto es exclusivo
PARA SOCIOS Y VISITAS
acompañadas de ESTOS

I love
the talk round a table
in the light of a bottle
of intelligent wine.
Drink up.
Remember, in every
golden drop,
topaz glass,
or purple spoonful,
that the autumn worked hard
to fill the vessels with wine;
and may the simplest of men learn
to remember the earth and what we owe it,
to spread the canticle of fruit.

Amo sobre una mesa,
cuando se habla,
la luz de una botella
de inteligente vino.
Que lo beban,
que recuerden en cada
gota de oro
o copa de topacio
o cuchara de púrpura
que trabajó el ontono
hasta llenar de vino las vasijas
y aprenda el hombre oscuro,
en el ceremonial de su negocio,
a recordar la tierra y sus deberes,
a propagar el cántico del fruto.

In my house, I have gathered together toys, small and large. I could not live without them. . . . My house, too, I built as a toy, and I play in it from morning to night . . .

En mi casa he reunido juguetes pequeños y grandes, sin los cuales no podría vivir...he edificado mi casa también como un juguete y juego en ella de la mañana a la noche...

In one part of the room, occupying a whole corner, there is an enormous shoe. It belonged to a shoemaker in Temuco. One day, we were going down a street close to the market when, suddenly, Pablo stopped, catching sight of this great shoe. I realized that the struggle to acquire it had already begun. We went closer, we looked at it, we smiled at the shoemaker, who did not even look at us, but went on working. "What a beautiful shoe you have there," Pablo said to him. He looked at us and, before we had said anything else, he warned us: "It is not for sale, it is not on loan, it's only there to be looked at." We laughed. In Pablo's eyes there was the look of a greedy child. "I'm going to leave my address and my name," Pablo said to him. "I would be very happy if you would sell me that shoe." He wrote down his name and we left. "We have to do something, Patoja," he said to me anxiously. The shoe was troubling him.

In the afternoon, I went back to see the shoemaker. I told him all about our house in Isla Negra, about the sea; I told him that Pablo loved things, and about how he cared for them. There this shoe would be much seen and admired. He said nothing. I invited him to the reading to hear Pablo, and I left him four tickets so that he could invite his wife and some friends. By way of farewell, he said to me, "Señora, don't waste your time."

We went back the following day. That gloomy and shy man who had scarcely looked at us was changed. He had become our friend. He welcomed Pablo and said to him, "I'd like to ask you a favor. Give me the book with your poem 'The More-Mother' and dedicate it to me. That will be the price of the shoe which is yours. You are the person who ought to have it."

—Matilde Urrutia

If I were able to speak with birds,
with oysters and with little lizards,
with the foxes of Selva Oscura,
with penguin representatives,
if sheep could understand me,
and tired woollen dogs,
and great cart-horses,
if I could discuss with cats,
if chickens would listen to me!

Si yo pudiera hablar con pájaros,
con ostras y con lagartijas,
con los zorros de Selva Oscura,
con los ejemplares pingüinos,
si me entendieran las ovejas,
los lánguidos perros lanudos,
los caballos de carretela,
si discutiera con los gatos,
si me escucharan las gallinas!

That horse was in a hardware store in Temuco. When Pablo went to school, he had to walk down that street, and he always noticed the horse and stroked its nose. He grew up seeing that horse every day, and thought of it as his. Each time we went to Temuco he begged the owner to sell it to him, but never with any result. Nor did his friends get anywhere with the owner. But one day the hardware store caught fire. The firemen arrived and, naturally, many people, among them friends of Pablo. Afterward they told us that there you could hear the single cry: "Save Pablo's horse! Don't let the horse burn!" And so it was saved—it was the first thing the firemen took out. Soon after, everything saved from the fire was auctioned off. The owner, who knew Pablo's passion for the horse, planted his own people to send the price up. He knew that Pablo would not let his horse get away, however high the price.

—Matilde Urrutia

On the four legs of my table
I unwind my odes.
I put out bread, wine,
and the roast
(black ship of dreams)
or I spread scissors,
cups, nails,
carnations, hammers.
My faithful table,
a four-legged titan,
bears up both
my dreams and my life.

Sobre las cuatro patas de la mesa
desarrollo mis odas,
despliego el pan, el vino
y el asado
(la nave negra
de los sueños),
o dispongo tijeras, tazas, clavos,
claveles y martillos.
La mesa fiel
sostiene
sueño y vida,
titánico cuadrúpedo.

His worktable in Isla Negra. When visitors come to the house for the first time, I show them this table and I say to them, "Pablo wrote his poems here—he was exceptionally fond of this table." They look at it, sometimes with surprise, sometimes with indifference. It's no more than a poor table. In the main, the people who visit the house don't see the things that Pablo loved most because these are the simplest, those of least material value. He loved and always looked for stones made smooth by the action of time. Roots fascinated him—he had many pieces of wood that he found in the forest. He told me they were small pieces of sculpture. This house was for him a dream universe. Only he understood the true value of his objects. I, as his shadow, understood also.

—Matilde Urrutia

They told me
many things, everything.
Not only did they touch me
and take the hand I gave them
but they were bound to my life
in such a way
that they lived in me
and were such a living part of me
that they shared half of my life
and will die half of my death.

muchas cosas
me lo dijeron todo.
No sólo me tocaron
o las tocó mi mano,
sino que acompañaron
de tal modo
mi existencia
que conmigo existieron
y fueron para mí tan existentes
que vivieron conmigo media vida
y morirán conmigo media muerte.

I sat in the garden, spattered
by the great drops of winter,
and it seemed to me impossible
that beneath all that sadness,
that crumbled solitude,
the roots were still at work
with no one to encourage them.

Me senté en el jardín mojado
por gruesas goteras de invierno
y me parecía imposible
que debajo de la tristeza,
de la podrida soledad,
trabajaran aún las raíces
sin el estímulo de nadie.

In my garden, it rests
from all of its sailings
over the lost oceans
that it pierced like a sword;
and little by little the creepers
will send fresh shoots
along its iron arms,
and in time carnations
will bloom in its earthly dream,
for it came here to sleep
and I cannot return it to the sea.

Now it will not sail in any ship.

Nor will it anchor save in my stubborn dreams.

En mi jardín reposa
de las navegaciones
frente al perdido océano
que cortó como espada,
y poco a poco las enredaderas
subirán su frescura
por los brazos de hierro,
y alguna vez florecerán claveles
en su sueño terrestre,
porque llegó para dormir
y ya no puedo restituirla al mar.

Ya no navegará nave ninguna.

Ya no anclará sino en mis duros sueños.

When, on September 11, 1973, the military in Chile rose to subjugate Allende's government, Neruda was ill, close to death, in the house in Isla Negra. Some days later, he was taken to a clinic in Santiago, where he died on September 23, his death forever synonymous with that of Chile. La Chascona, Neruda's house in Santiago, was sacked and vandalized; La Sebastiana in Valparaiso was also gone through by soldiers. The house in Isla Negra suffered some initial looting, but was then sealed by the military. Below the house ran a fence of flat wooden palings separating Neruda's land from the beach. With the house closed to them, people from all over have scratched tributes to Pablo, turning the house into a shrine.

—Alastair Reid

So, drawn on by my destiny,
I ceaselessly must listen to and keep
the sea's lamenting in my consciousness,
I must feel the crash of the hard water
and gather it up in a perpetual cup
so that, wherever those in prison may be,
wherever they suffer the sentence of the autumn,
I may be present with an errant wave,
I may move in and out of windows,
and hearing me, eyes may lift themselves,
asking "How can I reach the sea?"
And I will pass to them, saying nothing,
the starry echoes of the wave,
a breaking up of foam and quicksand,
a rustling of salt withdrawing itself,
the gray cry of sea birds on the coast.

So, through me, freedom and the sea
will call in answer to the shrouded heart.

Así por el destino conducido
debo sin tregua oír y conservar
el lamento marino en mi conciencia,
debo sentir el golpe de agua dura
y recogerlo en una taza eterna
para que donde esté el encarcelado,
donde sufra el castigo del otoño
yo esté presente con una ola errante,
yo circule a través de las ventanas
y al oírme levante la mirada
diciendo: cómo me acercaré al océano?
Y yo transmitiré sin decir nada
los ecos estrellados de la ola,
un quebranto de espuma y arenales,
un susurro de sal que se retira,
el grito gris del ave de la costa.

Y así, por mí, la libertad y el mar
responderán al corazón oscuro.

There is no space wider than that of grief,
there is no universe like that which bleeds.

No hay espacio más ancho que el dolor,
no hay universo como aquel que sangra.

Here
there is no street, no one has a door.
The sand opens up only to a tremor.
And the whole sea opens, the whole of silence,
space with its yellow flowers.
The blind perfume of the earth opens,
and since there are no roads,
no one will come, only
solitude sounding
like the singing of a bell.

Aquí
no hay calle, nadie tiene puertas,
sólo con un temblor se abre la arena.
Y se abre todo el mar, todo el silencio,
el espacio con flores amarillas;
se abre el perfume ciego de la tierra
y como no hay caminos
no vendrá nadie, sólo
la soledad que suena
con canto de campana.

Tyranny cuts off the singer's head,
but the voice from the bottom of the well
returns to the secret springs of the earth
and rises out of nowhere through the mouths of the people.

La tiranía corta la cabeza que canta, pero la voz
en el fondo del pozo vuelve a los manantiales
secretos de la tierra y desde la oscuridad
sube por la boca del pueblo.

We will win.
Although you don't believe it,
we will win.

ganaremos
aunque tú no lo creas,
ganaremos.

There's no forgetting, there's no winter
that will wipe your name, shining brother,
from the lips of the people.

Y no hay olvido, no hay invierno
que te borre, hermano fulgurante, de
los labios del pueblo.

So let no one be perturbed when
I seem to be alone and am not alone;
I am with no one and I speak for all.

Someone is hearing me without knowing it,
but those I sing of, those who know,
go on being born and will overflow the world.

Por eso nadie se moleste cuando
parece que estoy solo y no estoy solo,
no estoy con nadie y hablo para todos:

Alguien me está escuchando y no lo saben,
pero aquellos que canto y que lo saben
siguen naciendo y llenarán el mundo.

his face was formed in stone,
his profile defied the wild weather,
in his nose the wind was muffling
the moaning of the persecuted.
There the exile came to ground.
Changed into stone, he lives in his own country.

de piedra era su rostro,
su perfil desafiaba la intemperie,
en su nariz quebraba el viento
un largo aullido de hombre perseguido:
allí vino a parar el desterrado:
vive en su patria convertido en piedra.

I built the house.

I made it first out of air.
Later I raised its flag into the air
and left it draped
from the firmament, from the stars, from
clear light and darkness.

It was a fable
of cement, iron, glass,
more valuable than wheat, like gold—
I had to go searching and selling,
and so a truck arrived.
They unloaded sacks
and more sacks.
The tower took anchor in the hard ground—
but that's not enough, said the builder,
there's still cement, glass, iron, doors—
and I didn't sleep at night.

Yo construí la casa.

La hice primero de aire.
luego subí en el aire la bandera
y la dejé colgada
del firmamento, de la estrella, de
la claridad y de la oscuridad.

Cemento, hierro, vidrio,
eran la fábula,
valían más que el trigo y como el oro,
había que buscar y vender,
y así llegó un camión:
bajaron sacos
y más sacos,
la torre se agarró a la tierra dura
-pero, no basta, dijo el constructor,
falta cemento, vidrio, fierro, puertas-,
y no dormí en la noche.

"La Sebastiana"
(Valparaiso)

. . . They all left, the house is empty.
And when you open the door there's a mirror
in which you see yourself whole. It makes you shiver . . .

...se fueron todos, la casa está vacía.
Y cuando abres la puerta hay un espejo
en que te ves entero y te da frío...

our shoes on the stairs
awakened
other
ancient footsteps

nuestros zapatos por las escaleras
despertaban
otros antiguos
pasos

The day is not hour by hour
but pain by pain . . .

Hora por hora no es el día,
es dolor por dolor...

And at last the house surrenders its silence.
We enter and pace the abandoned rooms,
the dead rats, the empty good-bye,
water that wept in the gutters.
It wept, the house, night and day,
it groaned with the spiders, ajar,
it shed itself through its dark eyes

Y al fin la casa abre su silencio,
entramos a pisar el abandono,
las ratas muertas, el adiós vacío,
el agua que lloró en las cañerías.
Lloró, lloró la casa noche y día,
gimió con las arañas, entreabierta,
se desgranó desde sus ojos negros

Generals,
traitors:
see my dead house . . .

Generales
traidores:
mirad mi casa muerta...

The bedrooms were startled
when I cut through their silence.
There they were stranded
with their miseries and dreams;
for perhaps those who slept there
had remained awake.
From there they went into death,
the beds were dismantled,
and the bedrooms went down
like ships foundering.

Los dormitorios se asustaron
cuando yo traspuse el silencio.
Allí quedaron encallados
con sus desdichas y sus sueños,
porque tal vez los durmientes
allí se quedaron despiertos:
desde allí entraron en la muerte,
se desmantelaron las camas
y murieron los dormitorios
con un naufragio de navío.

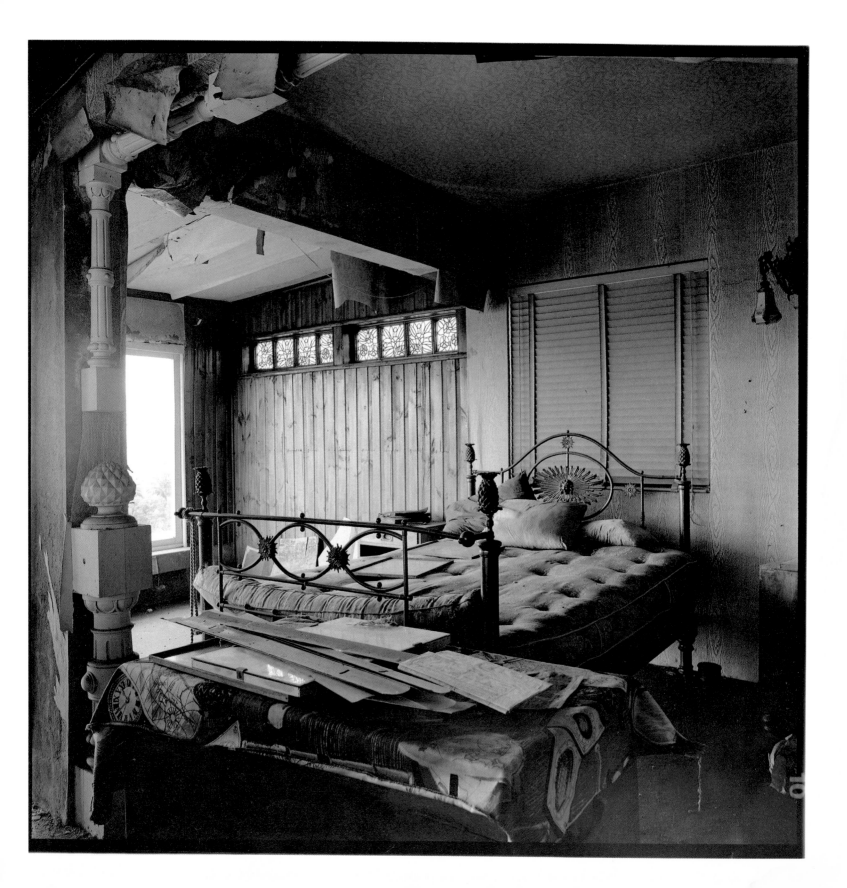

Stone, nails, planks, tiles, all
came together: here I put up
the tousled house with a running stream
that scribbled in its own language.

La piedra y los clavos, la tabla, la teja se
unieron: he aquí levantada
la casa chascona con agua que corre
escribiendo en su idioma.

"La Chascona"
(Santiago)

92

When they wish to see me, now they know—
they must look for me where I am not,
and if they have voice and time left over,
they can have a talk with my portrait.

Cuando quieran verme ya saben:
búsquenme donde no estoy
y si les sobra tiempo y boca
pueden hablar con mi retrato.

Todo tu cuerpo tiene
copa o dulzura destinada
            a mí.

Cuando subo la mano
encuentro en cada sitio
            una paloma
que me buscaba, como
si te hubieran, amor,
            hechos de arcilla
para mis propias manos de
            alfarero.

Los
versos
del
Ca-
pi-
tán.

The books
pile up. Fearful
pages that discourage
lion hunters.
Geographies
in four hundred volumes.
In the first ones,
there we full moons,
jasmine from the islands;
the last ones
are only solitudes:
snow kingdoms,
stirrings of reindeer.

Los libros
se acumulan. Terribles
páginas que amedrentan
al cazador de leones.
Hay geografía
de cuatrocientos tomos:
en los primeros
hay luna llena, jazmines de archipiélagos:
los últimos volúmenes
son sólo soledades:
reinos de nieve, susurrantes renos.

In the middle of the night I ask myself,
what will happen to Chile?
What will become of my poor, poor, dark country?

From loving this long, thin ship so much,
these stones, these little farms,
the durable rose of the coast
that lives among the foam,
I became one with my country.
I met every one of its sons
and in me the seasons succeeded one another,
weeping or flowering.

I feel that now,
with the dead year of doubt scarcely over,
now that the mistakes which bled us all
are over and we begin to plan again
a better and a juster life,
the menace once again appears
and on the walls a rising rancor.

En medio de la noche me pregunto,
qué pasará con Chile?
Qué será de mi pobre patria oscura?

De tanto amar esta nave delgada,
estas piedras, estos terrones,
la persistente rosa
del litoral que vive con la espuma,
llegué a ser uno solo con mi tierra,
conocí a cada uno de sus hijos
y en mí las estaciones caminaban
sucesivas, llorando o floreciendo.

Siento que ahora, apenas
cruzado el año muerto de las dudas,
cuando el error que nos desangró a todos
se fue y empezamos a sumar de nuevo
lo mejor, lo más justo de la vida,
aparece de nuevo la amenaza
y en el muro el rencor enarbolado.

It is time, love, to break off that somber rose,
shut up the stars and bury the ash in the earth;
and, in the rising of the light, wake with those who awoke
or go on in the dream, reaching the other shore of the sea which
has no other shore.

Es la hora, amor mío, de apartar esta rosa sombría,
cerrar las estrellas, enterrar la ceniza en la tierrra:
y en la insurrección de la luz, despertar con los que despertaron
o seguir en el sueño abrazando la otra
orilla del mar que no tiene orilla.

Some time, man or woman, traveler,
afterward, when I am not alive,
look here, look for me here
between the stones and the ocean,
in the light storming
in the foam.
Look here, look for me here,
for here is where I shall come, saying nothing,
no voice, no mouth, pure,
here I shall be again the movement
of the water, of
its wild heart,
here I shall be both lost and found—
here I shall be perhaps both stone and silence.

Alguna vez, hombre o mujer, viajero,
después, cuando no viva,
aquí buscadme, buscadme
entre piedra y océano,
a la luz procelaria
de la espuma.
Aquí buscad, buscadme,
porque aquí volveré, sin decir nada,
sin voz, sin boca, puro,
aquí volveré en el movimiento
del agua, de
su corazón salvaje,
aquí estaré perdido y encontrado:
aquí seré tal vez piedra y silencio.

# Remembrance

## DIEGO MUÑOŚ

In the summer of 1973, Pablo and I had a fifteen-day-long conversation. I was staying at El Tabo, easy walking distance from Isla Negra, and I would arrive every day just as Pablo had risen from his siesta. A bottle of whiskey was set out, with two glasses and a bucket of ice. We served ourselves and toasted one another.

The conversation began. We were actually running through our entire lives, not in any critical or introspective sense, rather like running a film. We would begin with "Remember so-and-so" or "Poor Somebody," and the people in question would appear in proper sequence. Sometimes one or other of us would start off as director, setting up a scene, and then the other with his particular lens would take it over. So we went on, playing back our own lives and those of dear friends, many of them dead. Sometimes we were helpless with laughter; just as suddenly we would taste a bitterness that would oblige us to drink our whiskey, ice and tears. But soon enough we'd be laughing again.

I saw with great clarity how the contradictions between the objective world and his subjective one brought about in Neruda the anguish that shows up in his poetry. The outside world had entered into his poems and come out transformed; or, more precisely, deformed. His world was also the world of his friends, difficult to understand and accept. For all of us, when we were young, the source and reason for our lives lay in love. We pursued it desperately. Fleeing the objective world, Pablo took refuge over and over in love, only to discover, disconcertingly, that once again would reappear just that world he was fleeing from.

Then he would join us in the bars and drinking places that were our refuge. In retreat from his solitude, he would come to us, only to discover himself even more solitary. But he loved being with his friends, for our company brought him back to life, revived him, and that brought him his greatest joy.

After that fifteen-day conversation in Isla Negra, as we were saying good-bye, he said to me, "Diego, this is the most important I've had in many years."

The sea helped us a lot in running through the long film of our lives, as it washed up endlessly on the sand; but the whiskey also played its part.

## JORGE SAURE

In those early days, I already had some reputation as a photographer, although only twenty-two; and that he was already known as a poet did not seem at all exceptional to me. It was in the house of a friend, Juan Gandulfo, that we met. We were on the patio, and Neruda said to me, in that slow, drawn-out voice, sounding of Temuco and the rainy south, "Jorge, take my picture." And that was the famous picture of him in a cape, reproduced so many times without any acknowledgment. I took it there and then, in natural light, for I never fussed about taking photographs. It was quite straightforward. I don't remember anything else. Perhaps because when we are young, we don't analyze our impressions, we just have them. Now that I am old, I study every new impression, for I am losing my edge, and perhaps not many new ones remain to me.

It was a meeting between a budding photographer and a poet well known from his very first poem.

## RAFAEL ALBERTI

On my visit to Chile in 1946, invited by him to give readings and talks, Neruda was certainly the most popular of poets, beloved by all classes of Chileans. He was living then in a vast house on the outskirts of Santiago, with a beautiful garden, half planned, half wild. During my stay, Pablo gave a number of parties there in my honor, always with the oddest mixtures of people—poets, of course, writers, politicians, painters, but also numbers of gate-crashers, people Pablo had never seen before. I will never forget, at the first of these parties, Pablo and me opening the kitchen door and seeing some strange-looking people with glasses of wine frying quantities of eggs in a huge pan. Pablo, amused and puzzled, signaled to me and we left silently. "They must know what they're doing," Pablo said to me. I've no idea who they are. They've never been here before."

Taking me by the arm, he led me away from the guests to a separate room, closing the door carefully behind him. There he served me a large glass of wine and himself a generous whiskey, and said, "I'm going to read you something that I think is quite important, that nobody knows about yet." And in his slow, sleepy voice, he read me the whole of "The Heights of Macchu Picchu," that great and essentially American poem which he brought back with him from the mysterious stone city in the clouds. The long and secret reading over, we returned to the party. The guests had multiplied visibly. The famous Chilean wines flowed freely, and everywhere the gentle cadence of Chilean Spanish, seductive and genial.

It was the first and last time I saw Pablo in his beautiful, brutalized country.

———

## JORGE BELLET

When I was working in Arica for an airline, Neruda and I would sometimes share a table in the only hotel. After his famous speech, "I Accuse!", in the Chilean senate, he had gone underground, and the plan was to get him out of the country. Throughout all this, Pablo was writing his *versaínas*. Do you know them? They were satirical poems, mimeographed and circulated every day. There was a serious move to capture and punish him. These daily needlings, besides, were very funny and politically very strong; they really went after the government's betrayal of the Chilean people. They tried to get him in Valparaiso and didn't succeed; they had a cordon around all ports and the beaches on the coast were watched. The Mexican ambassador tried to help him but was promptly declared persona non grata and obliged to leave the country. Someone with a strong physical resemblance to Pablo tried to cross at Curicó, and was detained.

At that time, I was in the south, in charge of a group of sawmills belonging to José Rodríquez, a rich entrepreneur. In the interior of Valdivia—in Hueinahue, on the edge of the Cordillera—we set up eleven sawmills which worked day and night turning out sleepers for European railroads. Quite by chance, in Santiago, I bumped into Victor Pey, who had been a passenger on the S.S. *Winnipeg* and who had at that very moment Neruda and Delia hiding in his apartment on Avenida Mackenna. After vacillating a bit, he told me the real problem in getting Pablo out of Chile.

There was one mountain pass through the Cordillera, known as Smuggler's Pass, which led to San Martín de los Andes in Argentina. I set as a condition a wait of some three months to prepare the way and to teach Pablo to ride in the mountains. Neruda was enthusiastic about this pioneering adventure, as were the officials of the Party—Lafferte Fonseca and Galo González. Manuel Solimano provided a car, which was modified for the roads of the south by Oscar Andrade, a racing driver who also had a job in the police laboratories. Without knowing what we were mixed up in, Oscar told me that the hunt for Neruda had high priority. I remembered Raúl Bulnes, Pablo's neighbor in Isla Negra, and for many years an army doctor. . . . The plan was ready. The car would go on ahead to wait with Victor Pey and a driver. They would be waiting for us at a crossroads in Graneros, feigning engine failure. We would leave—Pablo, Dr. Bulnes, and I. At the corner of the street, the duty policeman respectfully saluted the official flag the car flew.

In Futrano, we boarded a waiting launch; we crossed Lake Ranco to Llifén, where we took a jeep to Lake Maihue. At last, we saw the houses of Hueinahue. Pablo marveled at the landscape. The next day, he set himself to learn to ride, and in two months he could ride for four hours with no trouble. I was surprised by news of the imminent arrival of the sawmill owner, with his father and four Spanish businessmen. I went at once to some of the local bosses, to explain certain incompatibilities between Antonio Ruíz (Pablo's pseudonym) and Jose Rodríguez, the owner. Very generously, they made over quarters for Pablo. But Pepe, my boss, wanted to know what was up. I could only tell him the truth . . . he was happy to be of help in saving a man he admired.

In that hut, we spent four nights reading through *Canto General*, which Neruda had been finishing during his days. When these visitors had left, news came of another arrival: an official from the Ministry of Territories was coming to look into some claims against me, the day before our planned departure. The official turned out to be Victor Bianchi, a great friend of both of us who postponed his official mission to join our caravan.

At the end of our first day we were all on good terms, and we sat in a huge room with a fire burning, eating cheese and meat we had roasted. Pablo began to tell stories and legends of those parts. After a while we all sat in silence. As we were leaving, the proprietor said, "When you come with Don Antonio there's no charge here." The next day, we arrived at the pass through the Cordillera. Pablo asked its name, and at once began to improvise on it:

> How sweet the air is here
> in the pass of Lilela,
> never soiled, never,
> by the traitor González Videla.

We crossed a river. Pablo had a spectacular fall but was none the worse, And we performed a weird dance round a human skull, a custom among the few people that passed that way.

We arrived at San Martín de los Andes. For two days I wore riding boots and carried a whip in the hotel corridors, so that nobody accosted me. The only available telephone was in the military post, so, posing as a country squire, I had them help me put a call to Mendoza. The Party contact there took some time to understand the code I was using from the military post. That night, the officers gave us a farewell party. After about ten minutes, Don Antonio [Pablo] had taken over the conversation. They took him for some kind of secretary! Later that night he left for Buenos Aires. When the story of the escape came out, I lost my job. Twenty-odd years later, in 1973, I was arrested and interrogated about the details of that journey.

I was the only person granted the honor of going behind the bar with Pablo as he mixed drinks for his friends. Thus did he demonstrate a bond between us which he did not concede to others.

FRANCISCO VELASCO and
MARIA MARTNER

Neruda was already ill, and one day, after a long conversation by the sea, he asked me abruptly, "Do you believe in reincarnation?" I was very surprised, for the question had never arisen before in our conversations. "I don't know. What do you think?" "Well, maybe. . . . But if it is so, I'd like to be a bird, probably an eagle."

After Neruda's death, I was coming home one day when his housekeeper called to me in alarm, "Don Pancho, Don Pancho . . . there's a bird in Don Pablo's house!"

In the house, which had been closed up for months, a young eagle stared fixedly at us from among the rubble of the looting.

## EDUARDO GALEANO

I was in Isla Negra, in the house that was—that is—Pablo's. All entry is forbidden, by court order. A wooden fence surrounds the house. On it, people write their messages to the poet. There is not a scrap of the wood not written on. They all address him as though he were alive. With pencils or nail-points, each and all of them find a particular way of saying Thank you.

I also, wordlessly, found my way. I entered the house without entering. And in silence, we talked over wine, the poet and I, silently speaking of seas, of loves, of some infallible potion to cure baldness. We shared some shrimps in garlic, a huge crayfish pie, and other wonders of the kind that bring joy to the spirit and to the stomach, which are two names for the same thing, as Neruda knows well.

Several times we raised our glasses of good wine, and a sea wind touched our faces. It was all a ceremony to spite the dictatorship, that black shaft in his side, that mother-grief; and it was also a ceremony to celebrate life, beautiful and ephemeral as altars of flowers and passing loves.

## RAFITA

I knew him first in 1948. I worked for
him for more than twenty years; I built
most of the house, even the last part,
which he never saw finished.

To begin with, it was a house of only
two rooms, with a bathroom and a
kitchen. Every year he would add some
part. He would make drawings of just
what he wanted, whims of his, no right
angles, all with curves and odd shapes.

I put up the ships' figureheads. I
chiseled out the names of friends of his
who had died, which he had chalked on
the beams in the bar. He was very good
to me . . . he treated me like a son, not at
all like a workman, much more as a
friend. He had a way of putting things,
of conveying them, that was his alone.

I still look after the house.

---

## JOSE DONOSO

It seems to me that I have known Neruda all my life. I don't remember when I first met him—I imagine because I began to read him when I was a child. He had such an influence on me, or rather, he interested me so much. I read him passionately during my adolescence. This ancient memory I have of him probably comes from a connection between his family and mine, long before me. My uncles, the Yañez, were his first friends when he arrived in Santiago, and I think it was in their house, on Calle Dieciocho, that I first saw Neruda.

Later on, I think of Neruda in his own element; you might say. Neruda's element is very important: it was his houses. I think of him as a creator of ambiances, environments, as much as of words, environments made out of objects. His is a world of *materials,* materialist, if you like, quite closely connected to his poems. His fantasies are also material. The things that crowd his poems are things you can touch, almost see, almost smell. I think of him as a great creator of physical surroundings.

The first house of his I knew was on Avenida Lynch—a house full of his collections of things: bottles, books, toys. My wife has always said than when grown he collected all the toys he could never have as a child. I remember a bar decorated with turn-of-the-century postcards, a great novelty then. Now, everybody collects them, but then, thirty-five years ago, he was the first to notice them. This gift of his for seeing, for noticing things that others don't, was one of his great qualities. To see beyond the usual, to pick out objects, real or abstract, that only he noticed. This ability he had, to establish a relationship between himself and an object, between himself and a word, or between two words, and to collect such things, is essential to a creator, it seems to me. He was a creator in both the poetic and the lived sense.

I didn't like Neruda's houses. I found them ugly, but obviously they were houses of someone to whom surroundings mattered. That house on Avenida Lynch . . . the house at Isla Negra I thought horrible, but it was plainly the house of Neruda. Now, in perspective, I see it as ugly—but the first time I went there I found it wonderful. That was when I went to Isla Negra to finish my first novel. I was very poor, and I had six months in which to finish it. I lived in a fisherman's shack, with a tamped earth floor, but with a perfect view, beautiful, of rocks and beach. I had no bathroom, and took showers in Neruda's house. Both Matilde and Pablo were always warm and welcoming. Then I got to know him well, or he me, perhaps. There was always a gathering of people at weekends, of the "fauna." Neruda also collected people, people who outside of his circle were not at all extraordinary. He gave them an aura, a halo. They were "Neruda's." Just as he did with objects, with words—he endowed them with a kind of magic. He invented the *cantaritos* of Pomaire and Quinchamali—nobody would have given them a thought otherwise. He was the first to notice the poetry and the beauty in that modest clay.

His houses are not beautiful . . . they are Neruda, the products of his subjectivity, his being. He spoke of them so much that they became myth. He mythified, so that when one knew them after hearing so much about them, one was entering Neruda's aura, and saw them as rare. Now, without Neruda, they disintegrate and fall.

## JULIO CORTÁZAR

I remember the last time I saw him, February 1973. When I arrived at Isla Negra, it was enough for me to see his great door closed to understand with some extra-medical sense that Pablo had asked me down to say good-bye. My wife had hope to record a conversation with him for French radio; we looked at one another without speaking, and the recorder remained in the car. Matilde and Pablo's sister took us up to his bedroom from which he was carrying on his perpetual dialogue with the sea, with those waves which he had seen always as great eyelids.

In the evening, although we insisted on leaving so that he could rest, Pablo made us stay with him to watch a dreadful melodrama about vampire on television, which fascinated and amused him at the same time, as he gave himself up to a ghostly present which was more real to him than a future he knew to be closed to him. On my first visit, two years before, he had embraced me with a "See you soon," which had taken place in France. Now, he looked at us for a moment, his hands in ours, and said, "Better not to say good-bye, right?", his tired eyes already far away.

That was it. There was no need to say good-bye. What I have written represents my presence beside him, beside Chile. I know that one day we will go back to Isla Negra, that Pablo's people will enter through that door and will find in every stone, in every leaf, in every seagull's cry, the always-living poetry of that man who loved them so much.

# NICANOR PARRA

Ladies and gentlemen, I am no sudden Neruda fan. The whole question of Neruda has engrossed me ever since I learned to reason. No day passes in which I don't think of him at least once. I read him with close attention, I follow with growing astonishment his annual shifting in the zodiac, I analyze him, I compare him with myself, I try to learn what I can. I have also dedicated some quartets to him at dramatic moments in his life which was given over entirely to the cause of humanity. I have lived along with him for years, as a neighbor, as a pupil, as a sporadic visitor. Even more, we have exchanged objects and symbols: a copy of Whitman for a López Velarde, a piece of Quinchamalí pottery for an Araucanian poncho, a pocket watch for a garden of flowers and butterflies, etc. All of which gives me a right, I think, to consider myself a seasoned Neruda fan.

Even so, I react like a neophyte. Forgive my sincerity, but my state is like that of a recent graduate who has just been granted an audience with the rector of the university and who, with the nervousness of youth, forgets everything. I stammer and I lose my voice. My mind is a blank.

———

## ROBERTO MATTA

Yes, Neruda charmed us, but he was such a skeptic that I'm sure he was playing games with us all. . . . Pablo was a spellbinder, he had something of the comedian about him, he *was* a comedian . . . but Chaplin and Picasso were also comedians. How can one live if one is not?

Pablo was the image of despair. Art is like that. His despair was so vast that he had to interrupt it in the form of poems. He despaired of his shoelaces, of the illusions of the bottle, of the smell of Munñoz; he was always in despair. . . . One has to be in despair about everything, in order to defeat despair.

## ALASTAIR REID

I met him first in February of 1964. Jorge Elliot took me to his house in Isla Negra. Since I went barefoot, Pablo and Matilde called me ever after *el poeta patapelá*. Pablo was busy correcting the proofs of *Memorial de Isla Negra,* which was to be published later that year, his sixtieth, and he would read some of the poems to us at table, in that unforgettable voice of his. One afternoon, as he was handing me a sheaf of proofs, he said to me, "Why don't you translate some of these poems?" Seventeen years later, without Pablo, I translated the whole book.

I first translated *Estravagario* and *Plenos Poderes,* both books written in Isla Negra during that time Neruda called his "autumn," when all his worlds seemed to be in happy equilibrium. The translations gave us an excuse to talk frequently, about all kinds of things; but the translations themselves did not concern him much. One time, in London, he said to me, "I don't want you just to translate my poems; I want you to improve them." To know Neruda made a great difference in the work of translating his poetry, for his poems have above all a spoken intimacy of tone that I had to catch in English.

In the late seventies, my son and I were living on a houseboat on the Thames. When Pablo came to London, he made the boat his headquarters. He gave press conferences there, and held a birthday fiesta on board, in the course of which we had to fish a Ukranian poet from the river mud. Before he left, he read onto tape for me a variety of his poems, as a kind of translator's touchstone. I have played it over so many times that now I can hear it in my head at will; and with it comes back Pablo's whole aura, which stays in the air, and does not go away.

# BATUCANA

I fell in love with [Neruda's poem] "Farewell." So unexpected.

Ever since I was a kid I've had the same idea: that to be happy you shouldn't marry, because if you do, one person becomes the owner of the other, and so it doesn't matter how you treat them, well or badly, or if you are well treated, or please them or not—the poetry of love gets killed by laws. Then I read "Farewell" and find that this is a very big thing. It's not just something that my neighbor or her daughter tells me—it's the poet Pablo Neruda who says so. But then I find out that he has married, twice, the same woman, outside of Chile and again in Chile. I understand, if you marry outside the country it doesn't count here . . . but how could I not be interested in all this? Why go to all that trouble about marriage—not just marrying but marrying again, pleasing one kind of society and then another? Then I thought, How can this be? I just don't understand. It can't be!

And I was furious at Pablo, and I got married, although I already had a daughter. I get married and it goes badly and I put all the blame on Pablo Neruda, because I said, "I had decided not to get married!" I still loved his poetry, with admiration, with affection, with everything. Then I discovered that there's a lie somewhere in there. . . . Then I felt poetry was dead for me, it wasn't true, and anybody could make poetry; it wasn't its being true that counted, it was just something that happened. I was very depressed and sad.

Then about three years after I got married Pablo Neruda comes here and I decided to go and face him with my disgust about poetry. I went and I met him. He was flying a kite. At first I couldn't believe it could be him, for I knew him only from a distance, when he recited poems in Bustamante Park; then, suddenly seeing him up close, it was as if my guard had slipped, seeing him as just a simple *person,* flying a kite, just like that, quite real. He was really a man who spoke to people, who flew kites, moved the string this way and that, ran on the grass like everybody else. It was difficult to tell him off, but I told myself I had to, because that's why I went. I wanted to say to him first off, bluntly: "Look, if you thought that people didn't read your poetry or weren't moved by it or didn't take it seriously, you're completely wrong!" But I began to talk about "Farewell" and what I thought of that poem . . . and love, if love is a lie and you get married and . . . why had he married so many times? Then he laughed, pulled on the kite, handed the string to a child, gave me his hand, gave me a kiss, and told me that love was like trees: some loves shed their leaves, others are perennial. The perennials are not as beautiful as the ones that shed their leaves. So with love. It would go dry, then it would grow again, would be new again. It was the same as with all human things: they end and they come back. And it's quite normal that this happens to men and women at all ages, he said, and especially a person who feels things will fall in love many times. . . . Later, as years went by, I have realized that Pablo was so right . . . I couldn't really challenge him, but I did tell him, although I didn't raise my voice the way I'd meant to, no. He wasn't the kind you shout at, so open to talking. He talked right away, directly, quite serene, so easy . . . I thought he was going to excuse himself, but no! He went on speaking his poem, he didn't change . . . he used the same voice speaking to me as reading his poems . . . it was wonderful, that moment. . . . It so happened that the kite he had handed to the child came down and broke in pieces. Pablo asked for a piece, wrote his name on it, and gave it to me. On a piece of kite! I thought that was beautiful, and I kept it. His signature.

When time passed and I heard about his funeral, although I paid homage by myself, where I live, I grieved about not going to his funeral, I imagined it very solitary and sad. But then I found out that people came from all around the Recoleta and ran and ran and it was a big funeral. Right in the dictator's face, in the face of everything.

I still treasured my little piece of kite . . . but I don't have any egoism at all, and it came about last year that we had to find a reward for work some young people had done for our cause. Very difficult, but young people need a reward, an incentive. You can't ask young people to risk their lives for nothing, or just tell them, "Look, risk you life, but all we can tell you is someday we'll make our country free again." I gave the young boy the piece of kite.

He was very happy, the boy. More than that, he shared it with a girl and gave her a piece in public. . . . I don't have my piece any more, nor Pablo's signature, but I have this other wonderful thought. I know that, year after year, the piece of kite will go on dividing into more little pieces. I'm sure they'll go on giving away little pieces. . . .

That's all I can tell you, nothing more.

## JORGE EDWARDS

The astonishing success of his early lyric poetry annoyed him. "It's my worst poem," he complained whenever anyone mentioned "Poem Twenty" of his *Twenty Love Poems.* Even so, he went on to tell of a young couple in some provincial plaza in Colombia or the south of Chile, gushing to him: "Our joy began, in this very square, at dusk, in the spring of last year, with the reading of "Poem Twenty." Neruda smiled in satisfaction. "You see! I'm the matchmaker-poet!"

More of Neruda and "Poem Twenty": a reading in Lima, mid 1970, in a hall holding a thousand, full, young people on the floor, in the aisles, perched all around, only a small open space round the lectern. Time passed, and Neruda did not read his early love poetry. That kept up a kind of suspense. Suddenly, he turned a page and began, impassively "Puedo escribir los versos mas tristes esta noche..." In that vast hall, a deep sigh went up all around. Pablo took off his glasses and laughed, pleased, mischievous, as though he had been teasing the young people. He began again; and it was an extraordinary moment, one of intense vibration, of unforgettable communication. The whole audience rose and applauded deliriously. Neruda had to do an encore.

He could not conceive of human existence without the permanent state of being in love. Solitary people worried him; he found them incomprehensible.

He was famous for putting people in touch with one another, and helped bring together a number of couples. He took his role as matchmaker seriously. He thought of love as natural expansion, like breathing. As he thought of poetry. The only interruption of that natural respiration came with death, the incomprehensible phenomenon, the great scandal. Enigmatic solitude he saw as a sterile state, something close to suicide. He wanted to see the world as communication, as concert, as harmony, as a marriage of heaven and earth. The two halves of the apple of creation, one dark, the other light, had to end up in marriage, as he wrote in his memoirs. "Matchmaker-poet" was more than just a phrase or a joke.

## NEMESIO ANTUNEZ

Paris, 1952, the house of Alejandro Otero, the Venezuelan painter, a party on a summer evening. There was a single abstract painting in the room, large, all white, with one broad band of cobalt blue on its upper part. Neruda looked at it, somehow disturbed; then suddenly he took out his fountain pen, always with that emerald green ink of his, went over to the painting, looked again, and then wrote, horizontally, under the blue band: "To paint the sky, you must have your feet no the ground." Seeing this happen, the painter turned pale. We tried to calm him down, brought him a drink. . . . Then he smiled, and asked Pablo to sign his challenge. He recognized the fact that it had changed from being a contemplative work to becoming a backdrop.

Pablo was ahead of his time. Now, realism and abstraction go everywhere hand in hand.

A number of times I heard Pablo say that he was no intellectual, that stylistic analyses of his poetry drove him crazy. "I don't like to talk about poetry. I like to talk about food, wine, traveling, birds." How he loved to eat eel at Isla Negra, *piure* and *ulte* at Puerto Saavedra! The painting that really moved him was that of the primitives in New York museums. He stood a long time smiling and admiring Aduanero's *Sleeping Gypsy;* he passed cubists and surrealists with a frown. In Mexico, he would buy old still lifes, folk art, slices of watermelon with a blue pitcher, white wine in a crystal glass, sunlight falling on a table with a small, gray dead bird and a curtain. He loved old nineteenth-century oils of sailing vessels tossed by dark storms, he collected ships-in-bottles. In the Flora Norero in Valparaiso, we admired model steamships, their smoke made out of gray cotton, built by sailors in their hours of boredom, to end up on the mantle of that splendid restaurant.

Neruda painted his houses in blue and pink and other seaport colors. He was a surrealist architect. His houses grew year by year and harmoniously assimilated the poet's newest finds: the stuffed horse from his Temuco childhood, the balustrade from the Moneda Palace, the ship's figurehead from Liverpool, the paper flowers from Cuernavaca, the postcards with hearts and lovers, a locomotive in the garden, the dining room over a canal, the exterior staircase of shells which went up to the first floor of his house that clung to the top of a cinema on top of a hill, a drink with the poet in a fishing boat surrounded by pine trees, with a view of the sea and the horizon.

Neruda, we miss you badly! Chile lost its dazzle.

136

## MARIO TORAL

In Isla Negra, just when his new
workroom had been built, he said to
Matilde, "I need a desk, a special desk
. . . I don't know what, but it has to be
special."

Matilde made various suggestions—
windows, old doors—which he waved
aside. One day, looking out to sea from
the almost-finished room, he saw something that caught his attention.
"Matilde! Matilde! My desk! My desk!"

They both went down to the beach and
sat on the sand, waiting for a wave to
wash up the wood that was to be Neruda's desk.

## JOSE VENTURELLI

To collaborate with him was tremendously stimulating, for just as he believed in what he was doing, he projected that same belief into the work of others.

As for his passion for unusual objects, old things I would also like to have collected, although I could never have competed with the imagination and patience he pursued them with . . . he believed that things were charged with the presence of others—that is, an object had been lived with by other people, and something of the life of the other person remained in it, tangibly. Even broken things expressed something we should be in touch with.

Pablo saw these things in a perpetual motion and felt himself to be a kind of resting place for them, while they in turn would be changed by his presence.

We talked about this a lot—of how artists worked with insignificant materials: a painter mixes color which perhaps mixed differently would make only a mess, to be cleaned up quickly. . . . The materials we use are fragile—a stick with hairs on its point, a cloth, stripes of color—but a painter's intelligence and sensibility transform these things which come to him from somewhere else. He transforms them and transforms himself. . . . Then all this change in things is not something that goes away or disappears. In a certain way, it is contained in things themselves. . . . And here Neruda would move into a kind of imaginative irrationality. I remember one day, in China, we saw a lamp in a shop window. It was quite an interesting lamp, simple and elegant, we agreed, although to me quite ordinary. Neruda gazed at it, and then said to me, "When I set up my house in Rangoon, since I was weary of living so temporarily, I decided that what I most needed to change the order of things was a lamp, one that appealed to me. . . . One day I found it, and when I got home with it, there was a telegram for me announcing my transfer to another country. . . . That was both the end of my search and of a certain piece of my life. That lamp in the window is identical to the lamp I left behind in Rangoon so many years ago."

## CHARO COFRE and HUGO AREVALO

We had been in Paris since August 1972 without a cent. We were made welcome at the Chilean embassy by Neruda. September came, and he called together all the Chilean students at the Sorbonne, and made a proposal: "On September 18 [Chilean Independence Day], we are going to make this place into an inn. Bring branches." So that palace of an embassy, a landmark building, was transformed into a peasant inn. Following his instructions, we all gathered in the great entranceway and sang without stopping. A footman in seventeenth-century costume and white wig announced the arrival of surprised ambassadors, who were received by Neruda in a humble peasant suit, made over from his Nobel tailcoat.

Around Independence Day a year later, we heard rumors that Pablo was gravely ill, some said dead. Unthinkingly, given the dangers of the moment, we set out for Isla Negra to find out. . . . The memories of the previous eighteenth, in Paris, happy and unthinking, were still with us.

When we went upstairs we saw that his bed had been moved on the diagonal so that he could look out on the whole sweep of the sea. When he saw us, he said, "My children, I'm very ill, as never before; they call me from all over the place, and I can hardly move my hands. Stay with me, but bring your car in or they'll take the number, don't get connected with me, they'll go after you."

His own clandestine experiences and his time during the civil war in Spain prompted him to alert us to dangers we had never thought of. All the time, over television, came pictures of the coup, which, very upset as he was, he could hardly take in.

The next day, the telephone, which had brought calls from Italy, France, Mexico, and Sweden, was cut off. Around midday, in spite of his pain, he said, "We have to celebrate the eighteenth. Delia Dominguez brought me that red wine and we can fetch some empanadas from the inn."

Then over the television came more scenes that tormented him and increased the impotence he felt, a lucid mind in a gravely ill body.

"It's coming, I tell you—repression, a brutal repression." He spoke to his driver: "They'll arrest you eventually and torture you, but don't say anything. They might pluck out an eye if you answer them back. . . . The repression will be terrible, but then the people will reorganize."

By night, his pains had worsened. Going to our room we heard his voice: "This room is so cold. Can they bring a stove?"

Painfully, we felt it must be the end. Matilde woke us at five in the morning. "Pablo has had a terrible night. He's writing at this moment."

We never saw him again. We left in the wake of the ambulance that took him to the clinic, where he died a few days later. So did we live out his last day and his last night in Isla Negra.

## ALBERTINA AZOCAR

It was in 1920 that I met Pablo. I was studying French and we were classmates at the Institute. There were several poets there—I knew some of them, Pablo among them . . . Romeo Murga, a bright young poet who died of tuberculosis, Eugenio González, who became rector of the University of Chile, Roberto Mezafuentes, still alive, Raimundo Echevarría . . . they all got together on Saturdays and each would read his poems. . . . I heard Pablo read "Farewell" there and since Pablo has . . . had a sleepy reading voice, a friend of mine and I used to imitate him . . . that's how how we got to know and like him. After class, we'd walk on Avenida Cumming. I lived in Grajales, he in Echaurren, close by, and so we took to going together . . . that's how the "romance" got going . . . so long ago, imagine, I don't remember. . . . Then I was very sick, I went home to Concepción, my parents wouldn't let me return to Santiago because the same French courses had started up there, so then our letter writing began. Then he left, I didn't see him anymore. He went to . . . Rangoon, yes, as consul. We stopped writing—or rather he would write and I'd be lazy about replying. In 1929, the University of Concepción sent me to study in Brussels. From Paris I sent him a postcard telling him I was there. . . . I went in September, for about six months, for in those days the voyage from Panama took about a month going and about a month coming, so I was there about four months. He answered that I should go to him so we could be married. But those days, more than fifty years ago, you have to understand that things were not as they are now. I had to go back to my university, and besides that, my parents were fairly strict—I

didn't dare go. . . . He told me to change my ticket . . . but I didn't go. I went back to Concepción. When it was all over, he married. When he returned to Chile, he wrote again for me to come because he wanted to see me. I had a brother in Santiago. I went because in the last letter he had written me he was a bit upset about what I had done to him and he said . . . oh, he said a lot of things. What happened was that the director where I worked was an awful man. He opened the letter and asked me to explain everything on pain of being dismissed and all that. I told him he had no right to open anybody's letters and I resigned. I came to Santiago to work with a friend who ran a Montessori school and I lived with my brother. There, after a long time, we saw each other again. In that house I also met my future husband. After Pablo left for Spain, while he was abroad, I married the poet Angel Cruchaga. They were good friends. Pablo decided that Angel had been his master since college days and my husband worked in the Banco de España, where many writers visited him, Pablo among them. . . . When Pablo came back to Chile, he invited us to his house, and our friendship continued. We spent a lot of time in the house on Avenida Lynch, where Delia still lives, and we looked after it while they were traveling abroad. Afterward, when Pablo was a fugitive, he hid for a time in my house. . . . That's about all I have to tell you for now. Pablo was wistful, melancholy, in those student days, very thin . . . he looked ill, he was always delicate. . . . When we went for walks, he'd be silent, but I'm quiet too. . . . He wrote "I like it when you are silent" and also in a poem in *Residencias,* "Lamento Lento." . . . He lived very frugally, renting rooms with other friends in Calle Echaurren. His

father sent him money but he spent it who knows how. . . . He told me fantastic tales, he delighted me, he gave me French books . . . I must still have some of them . . . yellow bindings . . . Colette. . . . So many years I don't remember. . . . His verses are different from other poets'. . . .

---

## DELIA DEL CARRIL

Delia is the light in the window open
to truth, to the honeyed tree,
and time passed without my knowing
if there remained from our wounded
        years
only her shining intelligence,
the sweetness of the one who shared
the harsh room of my sorrows.

So, most gentle
passenger,
thread of honey and steel, who bound
        my hands
in the resounding years,
you exist, not like a vine laced
in the tree, but as truth, your truth.

I will pass, we will pass,
says the water,
and the truth sings against stone.
The course of the river spreads and
        shifts.
Wild grass grows
on the banks,
I will pass, we will pass.
So says night to day,
month to year.
Time
corrects the testimony
of winners and losers,
but the tree never rests in its growing.
The tree dies, another seedling comes
to life, and everything goes on.

Delia es la luz de la ventana abierta
a la verdad, al árbol de la miel,
y pasó el tiempo sin que yo supiera
si quedó de los años malheridos
sólo su resplandor de inteligencia,
la suavidad de la que acompañó
la dura habitación de mis dolores

Por eso, pasajera
suavísima,
hilo de acero y miel que ató mis manos
en los años sonoros,
existes tú no como enredadera
en el árbol, sino con tu verdad.

Pasaré, pasaremos,
dice el agua
y canta la verdad contra la piedra,
el cauce se derrama y se desvía,
crecen las hierbas locas
a la orilla:
pasaré, pasaremos,
dice la noche al día,
el mes al año,
el tiempo
impone rectitud al testimonio
de los que pierden y de los que ganan,
pero incansablemente crece el árbol
y muere el árbol y a la vide acude
otro germen y todo continúa.

## MATILDE URRUTIA

It was joy that Pablo loved; and for that reason, I'm not going to ask here that we remember him with a minute's silence. No—I'm going to ask for Pablo a minute of joy—a lot of noise, much applause . . .

Teatro Caupolocá.

I'm happy. At last I'm going to be with my Pablo . . .

5 January 1985, 3 a.m.

---

Matilde Urrutia, I'm leaving you here
all I had, all I didn't have,
all I am, all I am not.
My love is a child crying,
reluctant to leave your arms,
I leave it to you for ever—
you are my chosen one.

You are my chosen one,
more tempered by winds
than thin trees in the south,
a hazel in August;
for me you are as delicious
as a great bakery.
You have an earth heart
but your hands are from heaven.

You are red and spicy,
you are white and salty
like pickled onions,
you are a laughing piano
with every human note;
and music runs over me
from your eyelashes and your hair.
I wallow in your gold shadow,
I'm enchanted by your ears
as though I had seen them before
in underwater coral.
In the sea for your nails' sake,
I took on terrifying fish. . . .

Sometime when we've stopped being,
stopped coming and going,
under seven blankets of dust
and the dry feet of death,
we'll be close again, love,
curious and puzzled.
Our different feathers,
our bumbling eyes,
our feet which didn't meet
and our printed kisses,
all will be back together,
but what good will it do us,
the closeness of a grave?
Let life not separate us:
and who cares about death?

---

Matilde Urrutia, aquí te dejo
lo que tuve y lo que no tuve,
lo que soy y lo que no soy.
Mi amor es un niño que llora,
no quiere salir de tus brazos,
yo te lo dejo para siempre:
eres para mí la más bella.

Eres para mí la más bella,
la más tatuada por el viento,
como un arbolito del sur,
como un avellano en agosto,
eres para mí suculenta
como una panadería,
es de tierra tu corazón
pero tus manos son celestes.

Eres roja y eres picante,
eres blanca y eres salada
como escabeche de cebolla,
eres un piano que ríe
con todas las notas del alma
y sobre mí cae la música
de tus pestañas y tu pelo,
me baño en tu sombra de oro
y me deleitan tus orejas
como si las hubiera visto
en las mareas de coral:
por tus uñas luché en las olas
contras pescados pavorosos....

Alguna vez si ya no somos,
si ya no vamos ni venimos
bajo siete capas de polvo
y los pies secos de la muerte,
estaremos juntos, amor,
extrañamente confundidos.
Nuestras espinas diferentes,
nuestros ojos maleducados,
nuestros pies que no se encontraban
y nuestros besos indelebles,
todo estará por fin reunido,
pero de qué nos servirá
la unidad en un cementerio?
Que no nos separe la vida
y se vaya al diablo la muerte!

# Presence

## SELF-PORTRAIT

How to present oneself, to seem
human yet come out well? As when one
looks in the mirror or at a picture, trying
for the best angle (surreptitously), but
coming out always the same? Some people stand sideways, others intrude what
they want to be, others ask who they
are. But the truth is that we are always
watchful, lying in wait for ourselves,
pointing up only the obvious, concealing
the irregularities of our apprenticeships
and of time itself.

But let's get to the nub.

As for me, I have—or see myself as
having—a solid nose, small eyes, not
much hair on my head, a spreading
belly, long legs, broad feet, a yellowish
complexion. I am generous with my love,
hopeless at counting, clumsy with
words; with gentle hands, a slow walk, a
rustless heart; enthusiastic about stars,
tides, and sea storms; an admirer of
scarabs, a sand walker, bored by institu-
tions, a Chilean ever and always, friend
to my friends, close-mouthed about my
enemies, a dabbler in birds, awkward
about the house, shy in drawing rooms,
repentant for no reason, a terrible
administrator, an armchair sailor, an
ink merchant, discreet with animals,
happy under stormy skies, a prowler of
markets, withdrawn in libraries, melancholy in the mountains, tireless in for-
ests, slow of answer, witty years after,
vulgar all year long, sparkling in my
notebook, huge of appetite, a fierce
sleeper, at peace when happy, an inspector of night skies, an invisible worker,
disorganized, persistent, brave when
necessary, cowardly but not to a fault,
lazy by vocation, lovable to women,
active in suffering, a poet by ill fate, and
something of a fool.

## AUTORRETRATO

¿ Cómo arreglarse para parecer mal y
quedar bien? Es como cuando uno se
mira al espejo (o al retrato), buscándose
el ángulo bello (sin que nadie lo
observe), pero sigue siendo uno mismo
siempre. Algunos se plantan de soslayo,
otros imprimirán la verdad de lo que
quieren ser, otros se preguntarán ¿ cómo
soy ? Pero la verdad es que todos vivi-
mos acechándonos a nosotros mismos,
declarando sólo lo más visible, escon-
diendo la irregularidad del aprendizaje y
del tiempo.
Pero vamos al grano.
Por mi parte, soy o creo ser duro de
nariz, mínimo de ojos, escaso de pelos en
la cabeze, creciente de abdomen, largo
de piernas, ancho de suelas, amarillo de
tez, generoso de amores, imposible de
cálculos, confuso de palabras, tierno de
manos, lento de andar, inoxidable de
corazón, aficionado a las estrellas,
mareas, maremotos, admirador de escar-
abajos, caminante de arenas, torpe de
instituciones, chileno a perpetuidad,
amigo de mis amigos, mudo de enemi-
gos, entrometido entre pájaros, mal edu-
cado en casa, tímido en los salones,
arrepentido sin objeto, horrendo admin-
istrador, navegante de boca, y yerbatero
de la tinta, discreto entre los animales,
afortunado de nubarrones, investigador
en mercados, oscuro en las bibliotecas,
melancólico en las cordilleras, incansa-
ble en los bosques, lentísimo en las con-
testaciones, ocurrente años después,
vulgar durante todo el año, resplande-
ciente con mi cuaderno, monumental de
apetito, tigre para dormir, sosegado en
la alegría, inspector del cielo nocturno,
trabajador invisible, desordenado, persistente, valiente por necesidad, cobarde
sin pecado, soñoliento de vocación, ama-
ble de mujeres, activo por padecimiento,
poeta por maldición y tonto de capirote.

What could I say without coming to ground?
To whom would I turn without the rain?
Thus I was never where I found myself
and I took no journey other than the return
and I kept neither picture nor lock of hair
from the cathedrals—I have tried
to shape my own stone with the work of my hands,
sensibly, wildly, following my whim,
with rage and equilibrium—at every hour
I touched the territories of the lion,
the restless sanctuary of the bees,
thus, when I saw what I had already seen
and touched both earth and mud, stone and my foam,
natures which recognize my steps, my words,
curling plants which kissed my mouth,
I said "I am here," I stripped in the light,
I let my hands fall to the sea,
and when everything took on transparency,
under the land, I was at peace.

Qué podría decir sin tocar tierra?
A quién me dirigía sin la lluvia ?
Por eso nunca estuve donde estuve
y no navegué más que de regreso
y de las catedrales no guardé
retrato ni cabellos: he tratado
de fundar piedra mía a plena mano,
con razón, sin razón, con desvarío,
con furia y equilibrio: a toda hora
toqué los territorios del león
y la torre intranquila de la abeja,
por eso cuando ví lo que ya había visto
y toqué tierra y lodo,piedra y espuma mía,
seres que reconocen mis pasos,mi palabra,
plantas ensortijadas que besaban mi boca,
dije: " quí estoy ", me desnudé en la luz,
dejé caer las manos en el mar,
y cuando todo estaba transparente,
bajo la tierra, me quedé tranquilo.

O beautiful
is this planet,
full of
pipes
that hands
escort
through smoke,
of keys,
saltcellars,
in fact,
everything
made by
the hands of man,
every single thing,
the curve of shoes,
cloth,
the reappearance
of gold
without blood,
spectacles,
carnations,
brooms,
watches, compasses,
coins, the soft
smoothness of sofas.

hermoso
es el planeta,
lleno
de pipas
por la mano
conducidas
en el humo,
de llaves,
de saleros,
en fin,
todo
lo que se hizo
por la mano del hombre, toda cosa
las curvas del zapato,
el tejido,
el nuevo nacimiento
del oro
sin la sangre,
los anteojos,
los claves,
las escobas,
los relojes, las brújulas,
las monedas, la suave
suavidad de las sillas.

I am the Pablo bird,
bird of a single feather,
I fly in the clear shadows
and the confused light.
My wings are invisible,
my ears vibrate with sound
as I fly among trees
or underneath tombstones
like a sorrowing umbrella
or a naked sword,
formal as a bow,
or round like a grape.
I fly, I fly unaware
in the hurt of night.
There are those who expect me,
those who don't like my song,
those who wish me dead,
those who don't know I'm coming,
and who won't be out to get me,
to wound me, to misunderstand me,
or kiss my tangled feathers
with a whistle of the wind.
That's why I come and go,
but, flying or not, I sing:
I am the raging bird
in the quiet of the storm.

Me llamo pájaro Pablo,
ave de una sola pluma,
volador de sombra clara
y de claridad confusa,
las alas no se me ven,
los oídos me retumban
cuando paso entre los árboles
o debajo de las tumbas
cual un funesto paraguas
o como espalda desnuda,
estirado como un arco
o redondo como una uva,
vuelo y vuelo sin saber,
herido en la noche oscura,
quiénes me van a esperar,
quiénes no quieren mi canto,
quiénes me quieren morir,
quiénes no saben que llego
y no vendrán a vencerme,
a sangrarme a retorcerme
o a besar mi traje roto
por el silbido del viento.
Por eso vuelvo y me voy,
vuelo y no vuelo pero canto:
soy el pájaro furioso
de la tempestad tranquila.

I would come back from far away
in order to leave,
to leave again,
and I knew that to be a kind of dying,
going away while everything stays.
It's dying, with the Isla
flowering,
going away, with everything intact—
hyacinths,
the ship surrounding
the pale pleasure
of the sand
like a devoted swan.
Ten years which could have been a hundred years,
a hundred years without touching or smelling or seeing,
absence, shadow, cold,
and everything there in flower,
full of noises—
always
an edifice of water,
always
a kiss,
always
an orange,
always.

Yo volvía de lejos
para irme,
para irme de nuevo,
y supe así que así es morirse:
es irse y queda todo:
es morirse y la Isla
floreciendo,
es irse y todo intacto:

los jacintos,
la nave que circunda
como cisne abnegado
el pálido placer
de las arenas:
diez años que pudieron ser cien años,
cien años sin tocar ni oler ni ver,
ausencia, sombra, frío,
y todo allí florido,
rumoroso:
un edificio de agua
siempre,
un beso
siempre,
una naranja
siempre.

My heart has traveled
in the same pair of shoes,
and I have digested the thorns.
I had no rest where I was:
where I hit out, I was struck,
where they murdered me I fell;
and I revived, as fresh as ever,
and then and then and then and then—
it all takes so long to tell.

I have nothing to add.

I came to live in this world.

Mi corazón ha caminado
con intransferibles zapatos,
y he digerido las espinas:
no tuve tregua donde estuve:
donde yo pegué me pegaron,
donde me mataron caí
y resucité con frescura,
y luego y luego y luego y luego,
es tan largo contar las cosas.

No tengo nada que añadir.

Vine a vivir en este mundo.

I need the sea because it teaches me.
I don't know if I learn music or awareness,
if it's a single wave or its vast existence,
or only its harsh voice or its shining one,
a suggestion of fishes and ships.
The fact is that until I fall asleep,
in some magnetic way I move in
the university of the waves.

Necesito del mar porque me enseña:
no sé si aprendo música o conciencia:
no sé si es ola sola o ser profundo
o sólo ronca voz o deslumbrante
suposición de peces y navíos.
El hecho es que hasta cuando estoy dormido
de algún modo magnético circulo
en la universidad del oleaje.

Earth, give me back your pristine gifts,
towers of silence which rose from
the solemnity of their roots.
I want to go back to being what I haven't been,
to learn to return from such depths
that among all natural things
I may live or not live. I don't mind
being one stone more, the dark stone,
the pure stone that the river bears away.

Tierra, devuélveme tus dones puros,
las torres del silencio que subieron
de la solemnidad de sus raíces:
quiero volver a ser lo que no he sido,
aprender a volver desde tan hondo
que entre todas las cosas naturales
pueda vivir o no vivir: no importa
ser una piedra más, la piedra oscura,
la piedra pura que se lleva el río.

They will continue wandering,
these things of steel among the stars,
and worn-out men will still go up
to brutalize the placid moon.
There, they will found their pharmacies.

In this time of the swollen grape,
the wine begins to come to life
between the sea and the mountain ranges.

In Chile now, cherries are dancing,
the dark, secretive girls are singing,
and in guitars, water is shining.

The sun in touching every door
and making wonder of the wheat.

The first wine is pink in color,
is sweet with the sweetness of a child,
the second wine is able-bodied,
strong like the voice of a sailor,
the third wine is a topaz, is
a poppy and a fire in one.

My house has both the sea and the earth,
my woman has great eyes
the color of wild hazelnut,
when night comes down, the sea
puts on a dress of white and green,
and later the moon in the spindrift foam
dreams like a sea-green girl.

I have no wish to change my planet.

Continuarán viajando cosas
de metal entre las estrellas,
subirán hombres extenuados,
violentarán la suave luna
y allí fundarán sus farmacias.

En este tiempo de uva llena
el vino comienza su vida
entre el mar y las cordilleras

En Chile bailan las cerezas,
cantan las muchachas oscuras
y en las guitarras brilla el agua.

El sol toca todas las puertas
y hace milagros con el trigo.

El primer vino es rosado,
es dulce como un niño tierno,
el segundo vino es robusto
como la voz de un marinero
y el tercer vino es un topacio,
una amapola y un incendio.

Mi casa tiene mar y tierra,
mi mujer tiene grandes ojos
color de avellana silvestre,
cuando viene la noche el mar
se viste de blanco y de verde
y luego la luna en la espuma
sueña como novia marina.

No quiero cambiar de planeta.

I've been a great flowing river
with hard ringing stones,
with clear night-noises,
with dark day-songs.

He sido un largo río lleno
de piedras duras que sonaban
con sonidos claros de noche,
con cantos oscuros de día...

From so much loving and journeying, books emerge.
And if they don't contain kisses or landscapes,
if they don't contain a man with his hands full,
if they don't contain a woman in every drop,
hunger, desire, anger, roads,
they are no use as a shield or as a bell:
they have no eyes, and won't be able to open them,
they have the dead sound of precepts.

I loved the entanglings of genitals,
and out of blood and love I carved my poems.
In hard earth I brought a rose to flower,
fought over by fire and dew.

That's how I could keep on singing.

De tanto amar y andar salen los libros.
Y si no tienen besos o regiones
y si no tienen hombre a manos llenas,
si no tienen mujer en cada gota,
hambre, deseo, cólera, caminos,
no sirven para escudo ni campana:
están sin ojos y no podrán abrirlos,
tendrán la boca muerta del precepto.

Amé las genitales enramadas
y entre sangre y amor cavé mis versos,
en tierra dura establecí una rosa
disputada entre el fuego y el rocío.

Por eso pude caminar cantando.

Now we will count to twelve
and we will all keep still.

For once on the face of the earth,
let's not speak in any language;
let's stop for one second,
and not move our arms so much.

It would be an exotic moment
without rush, without engines;
we would all be together
in a sudden strangeness.

Fishermen in the cold sea
would not harm whales
and the man gathering salt
would look at his hurt hands.

Those who prepare green wars,
wars with gas, wars with fire,
victories with no survivors,
would put on clean clothes
and walk about with their brothers
in the shade, doing nothing.

What I want should not be confused
with total inactivity.
Life is what it is about;
I want no truck with death.

If we were not so single-minded
about keeping our lives moving,
and for once could do nothing,
perhaps a huge silence
might interrupt this sadness
of never understanding ourselves
and of threatening ourselves with death.
Perhaps the earth can teach us
as when everything seems dead
and later proves to be alive.

Now I'll count up to twelve
and you keep quiet and I will go.

Ahora contamos doce
y nos quedamos todos quietos.

Por una vez sobre la tierra
no hablemos en ningún idioma,
por un segundo detengámonos,
no movamos tanto los brazos.

Sería un minuto fragante,
sin prisa, sin locomotoras,
todos estaríamos juntos
en una inquietud instantánea.

Los pescadores del mar frío
no harían daño a las ballenas
y el trabajador de la sal
miraría sus manos rotas.

Los que preparan guerras verdes,
guerras de gas, guerras de fuego,
victorias sin sobrevivientes,
se pondrían un traje puro
y andarían con sus hermanos
por la sombra, sin hacer nada.

No se confunda lo que quiero
con la inacción definitiva:
la vida es sólo lo que se hace,
no quiero nada con la muerte.

Si no pudimos ser unánimes
moviendo tanto nuestras vidas,
tal vez no hacer nada una vez,
tal vez un gran silencio pueda
interrumpir esta tristeza,
este no entendernos jamás
y amenazarnos con la muerte,
tal vez la tierra nos enseñe
cuando todo parece estar muerto
y luego todo estaba vivo.

Ahora contarás hasta doce
y tú te callas y me voy.

I copy out mountains, rivers, clouds.
I take my pen from my pocket. I note down
a bird in its rising
or a spider in its little silkworks.
Nothing else crosses my mind. I am air,
clear air, where the wheat is waving,
where a bird's flight moves me, the uncertain
fall of a leaf, the globular
eye of a fish unmoving in the lake,
the statues sailing in the clouds,
the intricate variations of the rain.

Voy copiando montañas, ríos, nubes,
saco mi pluma del bolsillo, anoto
un pájaro que sube
o una araña en su fábrica de seda,
no se me ocurre nada más: soy aire,
aire abierto, donde circula el trigo
y me conmueve un vuelo, la insegura
dirección de una hoja, el redondo
ojo de un pez inmóvil en el lago,
las estatuas que vuelan en las nubes,
las multiplicaciones de la lluvia.

Give me, for my life,
all lives,
give me all the pain
of everyone,
I'm going to turn it
into hope.
Give me
all the joys,
even the most secret,
because otherwise
how will these things be known?
I have to tell them,
give me
the labors
of every day,
for that's what I sing

Dadme para mi vida,
todas las vidas,
dadme todo el dolor
de todo el mundo,
yo voy a transformarlo
en esperanza.
Dadme
todas las alegrias,
aun las más secretas,
porque si así no fuera,
cómo van a saberse?
Yo tengo que contarlas,
dadme
las luchas
de cada día
porque ellas son mi canto

Today you believe what I'm telling you.

Tomorrow you'll be contradicting the light.

I am one who keeps turning out dreams,
and in my house of feather and stone,
with a knife and a watch,
I cut up clouds and waves,
and with all these elements
I shape my own handwriting;
and I make these beings grow quietly
who could not have been born till now.

What I want is for them to love you
and for you to know nothing of death.

Hoy crees todo lo que cuento.

Mañana negarás la luz.

Yo soy el que fabrica sueños
y en mi casa de pluma y piedra
con un cuchillo y un reloj
corto las nubes y las olas,
con todos estos elementos
ordeno mi caligrafía
y hago crecer seres sin rumbo
que aún no podían nacer.

Lo que yo quiero es que te quieran
y que no conozcas la muerte.

Very well, this is the end of all my poetry has to offer you—for you, for today, for this after-noon, for tonight—and I leave you it for tomorrow. I don't know if it will put you in a thoughtful mood, this rambling poetry of mine. It gathers up earth and rain and fruit. Earth, rain, fruit, struggles, hopes—I leave you them, they're for you. Now I'm going—till tomorrow, till whenever, friend, companion.

From having been born so often
I have salty experience
like creatures of the sea
with a passion for stars
and an earthy destination.
And so I move without knowing
to which world I'll be returning
or if I'll go on living.
While things are settling down,
here I've left my testament,
my shifting extravagaria,
so whoever goes on reading it
will never take in anything
except the constant moving
of a clear and bewildered man,
a man rainy and happy,
lively and autumn-minded.

And now I'm going behind
this page, but not disappearing.
I'll dive into clear air
like a swimmer in the sky,
and then get back to growing
till one day I'm so small
that the wind will take me away
and I won't know my own name
and I won't be there when I wake.

Then I will sing in the silence.

De tantas veces que he nacido
tengo una experiencia salobre
como criatura del mar
con celestiales atavismos
y con destinación terrestre.
Y así me muevo sin saber
a qué mundo voy a volver
o si voy a seguir viviendo.
Mientras se resuelven las cosas
aquí dejé mi testimonio,
mi navegante estravagario
para que leyéndolo mucho
nadie pudiera aprender nada,
sino el movimiento perpetuo
de un hombre claro y confundido,
de un hombre lluvioso y alegre,
enégico y otoñabundo.

Y ahora detrás de esta hoja
me voy y no desaparezco:
daré un salto en la transparencia
como un nadador del cielo,
y luego volveré a crecer
hasta ser tan pequeño un día
que el viento me llevará
y no sabré cómo me llamo
y no seré cuando despierte:

entonces cantaré en silencio.

. . . I sing

I sing, I sing . . .

My gratitude to :

Matilde Urrutia
Pablo Neruda Foundation (Chile)
Alastair Reid
Cynthia Brown
Jaime Barrios
Jim Mairs
Susan Meiselas
Andres Poirot
and to all who generously helped me with this book, from
its birth in Barcelona 1982, through Paris, Santiago, and
New York in 1989.